TRAVEL SLANGUAGE

HOW TO FIND YOUR WAY IN 10 DIFFERENT LANGUAGES BY MIKE ELLIS

GIBBS SMITH
TO ENRICH AND INSPIRE HUMANKIND

Dedicated to Suzanne, Virginia, Mikey, and Phidgette

First Edition
20 19 18 17 16   5 4 3 2 1

Published by
Gibbs Smith
P.O. Box 667
Layton, Utah 84041

1.800.835.4993 orders
www.gibbs-smith.com

Designed by Katie Jennings Design
Printed and bound in Hong Kong

Gibbs Smith books are printed on paper produced
from sustainable PEFC-certified forest/controlled
wood source. Learn more at www.pefc.org.

Library of Congress Cataloging-in-Publication Data

Names: Ellis, Mike, 1961- author.
Title: Travel Slanguage / Mike Ellis.
Description: First Edition. | Layton,
Utah : Gibbs Smith, [2016]
Identifiers: LCCN 2015034945 | ISBN 9781423642336
Subjects: LCSH: English language--
Conversation and phrase books--Polyglot.
Classification: LCC PE1131 .E54 2016 | DDC 418--dc23
LC record available at http://lccn.loc.gov/2015034945
ISBN 13: 978-1-4236-4233-6

HOW TO USE THIS BOOK

If you've always been curious about how to communicate in other languages while traveling, but traditional methods seemed too complicated or time consuming, this book is for you! It includes twenty-six words and phrases translated into ten different languages that you can use to ask for help, introduce yourself to a new friend, or just find your way around. Follow the directions below and soon you'll be able to confidently navigate your way around the world.

- Follow the illustrated prompts and practice saying the phrase quickly and smoothly.
- Emphasize the words or syllables highlighted in red.
- A strikethrough means you don't pronounce that letter.
- Draw your own pictures to help with memorization and pronunciation.

Note: This book may produce Americanized versions of the various languages featured.

CONTENTS

FRENCH
Parles-vous anglais?

Par Lay Voo On Glade?

SPANISH
¿Habla Inglés?

Ah Blah'ing Glaze?

ITALIAN
Parla inglese?

Par Ling Glade Say?

PORTUGUESE
Você fala Inglês?

Vote Say Fall Lynn Glaze?

GREEK
Μιλάς αγγλικά?
Milás angliká?

Me Loss Song Glee Cop?

Sprechen Sie Englisch?

Spreck In Zee English?

Вы говорите
по-английски?
Vy govorite po-angliyski?

Vug Uh Vog Eat Tee

Pawn Glee Ski?

你会说英语吗?
Nǐ huì shuō yīngyǔ ma?

Knee We Shoe Ying

You Ma?

JAPANESE
英語を話せますか?
Eigo o hanasemasu ka?

Eggo Hand Us Say

Muss Cot?

KOREAN
영이 하시나요?
Yeong-eo hasinayo?

Young Oh Hussy
Nigh Oh?

I'M FROM AMERICA

FRENCH
Je viens d'Amérique

Chevy Ann Dam Air Eek

SPANISH
Soy de América

Soy Day Uh Mary Cup

ITALIAN
Vengo dall'America

Venn Go Doll America

8

PORTUGUESE
Eu sou da américa

Ew Sew Dot Mary Cop

GREEK
Είμαι από την Αμερική
Eímai apó tin Amerikí

E-mail Poe Teen

Ah Mary Key

GERMAN
Ich komme aus Amerika

Ick Come Mouse

America

Я из Америки
Ya iz Ameriki

Yes Ah Mary Key

我来自美国
Wǒ láizì měiguó

Woe Liza May Go

私はアメリカから
来たんです
*Watashi wa Amerika
kara kita ndesu*

What Tushy What

America Cod Ah Key

Ton Desk

저는 미국 에서 왔어요

Jeoneun migug eseo was-eoyo

John Noon Me Goop

Gay Sew Us Eye Oh

MY NAME IS...

FRENCH
Je m'appelle...

Gem Map Pell...

SPANISH
Me llamo...

Me Ya Moe...

ITALIAN
Il mio nome è...

Eel Me Oh No May...

PORTUGUESE
Meu nome é . . .

May Oh No Me Eh . . .

GREEK
Με λένε . . .
Me léne . . .

May Lay Neigh . . .

GERMAN
Mein Name ist . . .

My Numb Ma Ist . . .

RUSSIAN
Меня зовут . . .
Menya zovut . . .

Mean Yacht Saw

Vote . . .

我的名字是······
Wǒ de míngzì shì . . .

Woe Debt Mings Uh

She . . .

私の名前はです . . .
Watashi no namae ha desu . . .

What Tushy No Numb

 🎩

Eye Hat Day Sue . . .

제 이름은 . . .
Je ireumeun . . .

Chay Illuminate . . .

I DON'T UNDERSTAND

FRENCH
Je ne comprends pas

Shin Neck Come

Prawn Pa

SPANISH
No lo entiendo

No Low When Tee An

Doe

Known Cop Peace

Coat

Now Wean Ten Doe

**Then Cut Tail Of Vein
No**

GERMAN
Ich verstehe nicht

Ick Very Stay Uh Nicked

RUSSIAN
Я не понимаю
Ya ne ponimayu

Yay Knee Pony My You

CHINESE
我不明白
Wǒ bù míngbái

Woe Boo Ming Buy

JAPANESE
理解できません
Rikai dekimasen

Reek Eye Deck Key Muss Send

KOREAN
이해가 안
Ihaega an

E Hay Guy An

CAN YOU HELP ME?

FRENCH
FRENCH
Pouvez-vous m'aider?

Poo Vay Voo May Day?

SPANISH
¿Me puedes ayudar?

May P'way Daze Eye You Dar?

19

Me Poe Eye You Totty?

Poe Gem Me Eye

Shoe'd Are?

GREEK
Μπορείς να με βοηθήσεις?
Boreís na me voithíseis?

Bode Ease Numb May

Vote Thee Cease?

GERMAN
Kannst du mir helfen?

Con Stew Meer Elf An?

RUSSIAN
Вы можете
помочь мне?
*Vy mozhete pomoch'
mne?*

Vim Most Tape Pom Osh Minnie?

CHINESE
你能帮助我吗?
*Nǐ néng bāngzhù
wǒ ma?*

Knee Nung Bong Zoo Woe Ma?

JAPANESE
手伝って頂けますか？
*Tetsudatte
itadakemasu ka?*

Tet Sue Dot Tate Todd

●

Dock Kay Muss Cot?

KOREAN
도와주실 수 있으세요?
Dowajusil su isuseyo?

D'Why Jean She See

Sue Say Ow

I'M LOST

FRENCH
Je suis perdu

Jess We Pear Due

SPANISH
Estoy perdido

Ace Toy Pear Dee Doe

ITALIAN
Mi sono perso

Me Sew No Pear Sew

PORTUGUESE
Estou perdido

Ease Toe Pear Jean Doe

GREEK
Έχω χαθεί
Écho chatheí

Echo **Cat** Thee

GERMAN
Ich bin verloren

Ick **Bin Fair** Lauren

RUSSIAN
Я заблудился
Ya zabludilsya

Yacht **Sub Blue**

Deals Yacht

CHINESE
我迷路了
Wǒ mílùle

Woe Me Lou Lot

JAPANESE
道に迷いました
Michi ni mayoi mashita

Me She Knee My Oh

E Mush Top

KOREAN
길을 잃었어요
Gileul ireoseoyo

Key Ray Eat Us Eye Oh

PLEASE

FRENCH *S'il vous plaît*	 See Voo Play
SPANISH *Por favor*	 Pour Fun Vor
ITALIAN *Per favore*	Pear Fun Vor Ray

PORTUGUESE
Por favor

Pour Fun Vor

GREEK
Παρακαλώ
Parakaló

Pod Dock Call Oh

GERMAN
Bitte

Bitter

RUSSIAN
Пожалуйста
Pozhaluysta

Patch Al Step

CHINESE
请
Qǐng

Cheeng

Oh Neigh Guy She Must

Has Say Ow

THANK YOU

FRENCH
Merci

 Mare See

SPANISH
Gracias

Grassy Us

ITALIAN
Grazie

Grotto See

PORTUGUESE
Obrigado

Oh Bree God Doe

GREEK
Ευχαριστώ
Efcharistó

Elf Coddy Stow

GERMAN
Danke

Dunk Ah

RUSSIAN
Спасибо
Spasibo

Spa See Bop

CHINESE
谢谢
Xièxiè

Shay Shay

Oddy Got Toe

Comb Mop Sunny

Dad

YOU'RE WELCOME

FRENCH
De rien
Durry ~~Ann~~

SPANISH
De nada
Day Nod Ah

ITALIAN
Prego
Pray Go

PORTUGUESE
De nada

June Odd Duh

GREEK
Παρακαλώ
Parakaló

Pod Dock Call Oh

GERMAN
Gern geschehen

Gary'n Gush Sheen

RUSSIAN
Пожалуйста
Pozhaluysta

Patch Al Step

CHINESE
不客气
Bù kèqì

Book Itchy

JAPANESE
どういたしまして
Dōitashimashite

Doe Eat Tushy Mush

Tape

KOREAN
별 말씀을
Byeol malsseumeul

Pull Mice Mail

EXCUSE ME

FRENCH
Excusez-moi

Ex Coos Aim Wog

SPANISH
Disculpa

Dis Cool Pa

ITALIAN
Scusami

Schools Ah Me

PORTUGUESE
Desculpe

Desk Cold Pay

GREEK
Συγνώμη
Sygnómi

Sing Uh No Me

GERMAN
Entschuldigung

End School Dee Gun

RUSSIAN
Извините
Izvinite

Is Vee Knee Tip

CHINESE
劳驾
Láojià

Low Jab

JAPANESE
すみません
Sumimasen

KOREAN
실례합니다
Sillye habnida

Sue Me Mustn't

She'll Lay Uh Knee

● Dot

CHEERS!

FRENCH
Santé!   Saw Tape

SPANISH
¡Salud!   Sal Lude

ITALIAN
Salute!   Sal Loot Tape

PORTUGUESE
Saúde!

Sow Jean

GREEK
Στην υγειά σου!
St<u>in</u> ygeiá sou!

Stint Yee Guess Sew

GERMAN
Prost!

P'Roast

RUSSIAN
На здоровье!
Na zdorov'ye!

Nuts Da Rove Yeah

CHINESE
干杯!
Gānbēi!

Chin Bay

JAPANESE
乾杯!
Kanpai

Con Pie

KOREAN
건배!
Geonbae!

Con Bay

NICE TO MEET YOU

FRENCH
Enchanté

On Shawn Tape

SPANISH
Mucho gusto

Mooch Oh Goose Toe

ITALIAN
Piacere di conoscerla

Pea Yacht Shed Dee

Cone Oh Share La

PORTUGUESE
Muito prazer

Moo E 2 Brassiere

GREEK
Χάρηκα για τη γνωριμία
Chárika gia ti gnorimía

Car Got Yacht Tee

Norm Me Ah

GERMAN
Nett, dich zu treffen

Net Dick Zoo Tref Fin

Приятно
познакомиться
*Priyatno
poznakomit'sya*

Pre Yacht No Pose

Knock Comb It's Ah

很高兴认识你
Hěn gāoxìng rènshí nǐ

Hun Gown Shing

Rent She Knee

始めまして
Hajimemashite

Hadji May Mush Tape

만나서 반갑습니다
*Mannaseo
bangabseubnida*

Man As Sew Pan Gob

Sue Knee Dad

I NEED A TAXI

FRENCH
Je besoin d'un taxi

Jug Buzz Wand Dunk Taxi

SPANISH
Necesito un taxi

Neigh Say See Toe

~~Moon~~ Taxi

45

Oh Bee Zone Yo Dee

Moon Taxi

Ew Pray See Sue Dee

You'm Taxi

Χρειάζομαι ένα ταξί
Chreiázomai éna taxí

Cleedy Oz Oh Main Nut Taxi

Ich brauche ein Taxi

Ick Brow Huh Eye'n Taxi

Мне нужно такси
Mne nuzhno taksi

Me Ann News Shut No Taxi

我需要一辆出租车
Wǒ xūyào yī liàng chūzū chē

Wo See Yow Ying Young Chew Zoo Chef

JAPANESE
私はタクシー
を必要とします
*Watashi wa takushī o
hitsuyō to shimasu*

What Tushy What

Tock She Oh Heats

See You Toe She Muss

Nan Noon Tuck She

KOREAN
나는 태시를 필요
*Naneun taegsileul
pil-yo*

Lee Pea Lee Yo

I NEED A DOCTOR

FRENCH
J'ai besoin d'un médecin

Jay Buzz When Dunk

Made Sank

SPANISH
Necesito un médico

Neigh Say See Toe

Tune May Dee Comb

Oh Bee Sewn Yo

D'You'n Due Tory

Pray See Sue Geo

Magic Oh

Χρειάζομαι ένα γιατρό
Chreiázomai éna giatró

Cheery Oz Oh May

Neigh Yet Row

Ich brauche einen Arzt

Ick Brow Huh Eye'n

In Arts't

RUSSIAN
Мне нужен доктор
Mne nuzhen doktor

M'Knee Uh News
Shun Doctor

CHINESE
我需要一个医生
Wǒ xūyào yīgè yīshēng

Woe She Ow Yee
Gut Yee Shung

JAPANESE
医者に診てもらい
たいのですが
*Isha ni mite moraitai
no desuga*

Each And Knee Meat

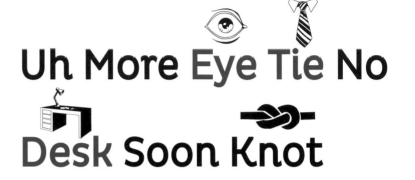

Uh More Eye Tie No

Desk Soon Knot

KOREAN
의사가 필요 해요
Uisaga pil-yo haeyo

We Saw Gop Peal
You Ow

CALL AN AMBULANCE

FRENCH
Appelez une ambulance

Apple Lay Nom Boo Lawns

SPANISH
Llama una ambulancia

Yam Eh Moon Am

 Boo Lance See Ya

ITALIAN
Chiami un'ambulanza

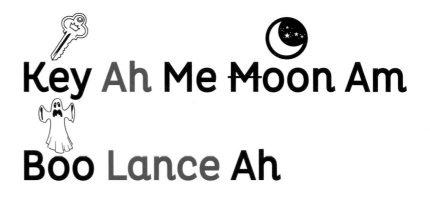

Key Ah Me Moon Am

Boo Lance Ah

PORTUGUESE
Chame uma ambulância

Sham May Ooh

Mumble Ann See Ya

Καλέστε ένα
ασθενοφόρο
Kaléste éna asthenofóro

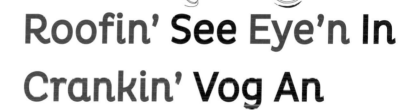

Call Less Ten Us Ten

Oh **Photo**

*Rufen Sie einen
Krankenwagen*

Roofin' See Eye'n In

Crankin' **Vog An**

Вызовите скорую

Vyzovite skoruyu

V'Wheeze Uh Vee Tess Code Ooh

打电话叫救护车

Dǎ diànhuà jiào jiùhù chē

Dot Dee Wow Jowł

Jew Who Shoe

救急車を呼んでください
*Kyūkyūsha wo
yondekudasai*

Cue Cue Shower
Young Day Could
Decide

구급차를 불러 주세요
*Gugeubchareul bulleo
juseyo*

Goo Goop Char Ray
Pull Oh Jess Hey Ow

NICE HOTEL

FRENCH
Bel hôtel

Bell Oh Tell

SPANISH
Bonito hotel

Bow Knee Toe Tell

ITALIAN
Bell'hotel

Bell Oh Tell

PORTUGUESE
Bom hotel

Bow Moe Tell

GREEK
Ωραίο ξενοδοχείο
Oraío xenodocheío

Ode Eye Oxen Oh

Doe Heel

GERMAN
Schönes Hotel

Sure Ness Oh Tell

RUSSIAN
Хороший отель
Khoroshiy otel'

Cuddle Chateau Tay

NICE HOTEL **61**

Boot Sew Day Show Dean

Stay Key Knot Hoe Tay Due

Joan Hoe Tell

THE HOSPITAL

FRENCH
L'hôpital

Low Pea Tale

SPANISH
El hospital

Elk Lows Pea Tale

ITALIAN
L'ospedale

Low Spay Dolly

PORTUGUESE
O hospital

Woe Spit Tale

GREEK
Το νοσοκομείο
To nosokomeío

Toe No Soak Oh Me Oh

GERMAN
Das Krankenhaus

Dusk Crunkin' House

RUSSIAN
Больница
Bol'nitsa

Ball Neats Ah

CHINESE
该医院
Gāi yīyuàn

Guy Yee When

JAPANESE
病院
Byōin

Bee Yo Yeen

KOREAN
병원
Byeong-won

P'Young Won

ROOM NUMBER

FRENCH
Numéro de chambre

New Mare Oh Duh

Shawn Bra

SPANISH
Número de habitación

New Mare Oh Day

Hobby Tah See Own

66

ITALIAN
Numero di stanza

New Mare Oh Dee Stance Ah

PORTUGUESE
Número do quarto

New Maid Oh Due Quart Oh

ROOM NUMBER 67

Αριθμόσ δωματίου
Arithmós dọmatíou

Alice Most Doe Ma Teal

Zimmernummer

Simmer New Mar

Номер комнаты
Nomer komnaty

No Murk Comb Naughty

CHINESE
房间号
Fángjiān hào

Fun Jean How

JAPANESE
部屋番号
Heya bangō

Hey Up Bang Go

KOREAN
방 번호
Bang beonho

Pan Bun Hòe

THE AIRPORT

FRENCH
L'aéroport

Lay Rope Or

SPANISH
El aeropuerto

El Lay Dope Where

Toe

ITALIAN *L'aeroporto*	Lied Oh Pour Toe
PORTUGUESE *O aeroporto*	Oh Ed Oh Pour Toe
GREEK Το αεροδρόμιο *To aerodrómio*	2 Ed Oh D'Romeo
GERMAN *Der Flughafen*	Dare Fluke Huffin'
RUSSIAN Аэропорт *Aeroport*	Ed Ah Port

CHINESE
飞机场
Fēijī chǎng

Fay Jean Chung

JAPANESE
空港
Kūkō

Kook Oh

KOREAN
공항
Gonghang

Goon Hang

BUS STATION

FRENCH
Arrêt de bus

Arrayed Booze

SPANISH
Estación de autobus

Ace Top See Own

Day Out Toe Booze

ITALIAN
Stazione degli autobus

Stott See Own Ned

Dee Out Toe Booze

PORTUGUESE
Rodoviária

Road Oh Vee Oddy Ah

GREEK
Στάση λεωφορείου
Stási leoforeíou

Stop Say Loaf 4 You

GERMAN
Bushaltestelle

Bus Halt Tess Stella

RUSSIAN Автовокзал *Avtovokzal*	**After Vog Sell**
CHINESE 公车站 *Gōngchē zhàn*	**Gong Chew Jen**
JAPANESE バス停 *Basutei*	**Bus Tay**
KOREAN 버스 정류장 *Beoseu jeonglyujang*	**Bow Sue Chung You Dang**

FRENCH
Police

Police

SPANISH
Policía

Poe Lee See Ya

ITALIAN
Polizia

Pole Eat See Ya

PORTUGUESE
Polícia

Poe Lee See Ya

GREEK
Αστυνομία
Astynomía

As Tee No Me Uh

GERMAN
Polizei

Pole Eats Eye

RUSSIAN
Полиция
Politsiya

Pole Eats Say

CHINESE
警察
Jǐngchá

Jing Chop

JAPANESE
警察
Keisatsu

Kay Sats Sue

KOREAN
경찰
Gyeongchal

Gong Chime

AMERICAN EMBASSY

FRENCH
Ambassade américaine

Ump Bus Sod Ah
Mary Ken

SPANISH
Embajada americana

Aim Bah Hotta Ah
Mary Con Ah

ITALIAN
Ambasciata americana

Ump Bus Shot Tom
Eddie Con **Ah**

PORTUGUESE
Embaixada americana

Aim By Shod **Uh**
Meddy Coon **Ah**

Αμερικανική πρεσβεία
Amerikanikí presveía

Ah Mary Connie Key Press Vee Ah

Amerikanische Botschaft

Ah Mary Con Is

Should Boat Shaft

RUSSIAN
Американское
посольство
Amerikanskoye
posol'stvo

Ah Meddy Con Skate

Bus Soy Stop

CHINESE
美国大使馆
Měiguó dàshǐ guǎn

May Go Dash Sheik One

JAPANESE
アメリカ大使館
Amerika taishikan

Ah Meddy Cot Tie Sh'Con

KOREAN
미국 대사관
Migug daesagwan

Me Goog Day Sock When

GOOD RESTAURANT

FRENCH
Bon restaurant

Bone Rest Oh Ron

SPANISH
Buen restaurante

B'Wayne Rest Oh Ron Tay

ITALIAN
Buon ristorante

Bone Rest Or Ron Tay

PORTUGUESE
Bom restaurante

Bomb Rest Oh Ranchy

GREEK
Καλό εστιατόριο
Kaló estiatório

Call Oh West Tee Ah

Toady Oh

GERMAN
Gutes Restaurant

Goo Tess Rest Oh Ron

Хороший ресторан
Khoroshiy restoran

Code Oh She Wrist
Ah Ron

CHINESE
好的餐厅
Hǎo de cāntīng

How Duh Sun Ching

JAPANESE
良いレストラン
Yoi resutoran

Yo E Rest Oh Ron

KOREAN
좋은 식당
Joeun sikdang

Joan Sheik Dang

86 GOOD RESTAURANT

HOW MUCH?

FRENCH
Combien?

Comb Bee Yawn?

SPANISH
¿Cuánto?

Kwan Toe?

ITALIAN
Quanto?

Kwan Toe?

PORTUGUESE
Quanto?

Kwan Toe?

GREEK
Πόσο?
Póso?

Poe Sew?

GERMAN
Wie viel?

Vee Feel?

RUSSIAN
Сколько?
Skol'ko?

Skull Ka?

CHINESE
多少钱?
Duōshǎo qián?

Due Shower Chin?

JAPANESE
いくらですか?
Ikuradesu ka?

Ick Coo'd Ah Desk

 Cot

KOREAN
얼마에요?
Eolma-eyo?

Ol' Ma Ay Yo?

THE CHECK, PLEASE

Less Sheck See Voo

 Play

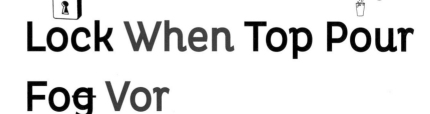 Lock When Top Pour

Fog Vor

Eel Cone Toe Pear Fog Voe Day

Ah Cone Top Pour Fog Vor

Τον λογαριασμό,
παρακαλώ
Ton logariasmó,
parakaló

Tone Logger Yes Moe

Pair Uh Call Low

Die Rechnung, bitte

Dee Wreck Noon

Bitter

Счет пожалуйста
Schet, pozhaluysta

Shoot Poe Shawls Tap

请买单
Qǐng maidan

Ching My Done

お勘定をお願いします
Okanjō wō onegaishimasu

Oak And Joe Oh

Neigh Guy She Muss

계산서 주세요
Gyesanseo juseyo

Key Sang Sew Juice

Hay Oh

FRENCH
Je payerai

Jug Payer Eh

SPANISH
Yo pagaré

Yo Pog God Ay

ITALIAN
Vorrei pagare

Voo Ray Pog God Ay

PORTUGUESE
Vou pagar

Voo Pog Are

GREEK
Θα πληρώσω
Tha pliróso

The Plead Oh Sew

GERMAN
Ich werde bezahlen

Ick Very Duh Bets All In

RUSSIAN
Я заплачу
Ya zaplachu

Yeah Zap Lie Shoe

我会付
Wǒ huì fù

Woe Way Food

私が払います
Watashi ga haraimasu

What Tushy God

Hot Eye Muss

내가 지불
Naega jibul

Neck Guy She Pool